1-2-3
My Feelings and Me

Goldie Millar and Lisa A. Berger

Illustrated by Priscilla Burris

free spirit
PUBLISHING®

Text copyright © 2019 Goldie Millar and Lisa Berger
Illustrations copyright © 2019 Free Spirit Publishing

Library of Congress Cataloging-in-Publication Data
Names: Millar, Golden Melanie, 1972– author. | Berger, Lisa, 1967– author. | Burris, Priscilla, illustrator.
Title: 1-2-3 my feelings and me / by Goldie Millar and Lisa A. Berger ; illustrated by Priscilla Burris.
Other titles: One, two, three my feelings and me
Description: Minneapolis, Minnesota : Free Spirit Publishing Inc., [2019]
Identifiers: LCCN 2018056292 | ISBN 9781631983627 (hardcover) | ISBN 1631983628 (hardcover)
Subjects: LCSH: Emotions in children—Juvenile literature. | Emotions—Juvenile literature.
Classification: LCC BF723.E6 M55 2019 | DDC 155.4/124—dc23 LC record available at https://lccn.loc.gov/2018056292

Free Spirit Publishing does not have control over or assume responsibility for author or third-party websites and their content.

Edited by Alison Behnke
Cover and interior design by Shannon Pourciau

Printed in China

Free Spirit Publishing
An imprint of Teacher Created Materials
6325 Sandburg Road, Suite 100
Minneapolis, MN 55427-3674
(612) 338-2068
help4kids@freespirit.com
freespirit.com

Dedication

To each other for the friendship, support, sharing, and meaningful work!

A Letter to Caring Adults

Welcome, everyone! We are so glad you have found this book. Parents, grandparents, teachers, counselors, and all caring adults play an important role in helping children with their feelings.

Understanding how feelings work and what to do with them is a skill that children can learn and practice. Children who understand, accept, and manage their feelings in healthy ways experience greater overall emotional and physical wellness.

This book gives you friendly, straightforward, and hands-on ways to support children in identifying, expressing, and coping with all their feelings. This is done in child-friendly language, structured around a counting format, which is easy to remember and integrate into your busy life. The Guide for Caring Adults at the back of the book contains even more information, ideas, and easy-to-use strategies. *1-2-3 My Feelings and Me* is meant to be read, shared, discussed, and played with!

We hope that together you will have fun, learn, and feel empowered.

Yours on the feeling journey,
—Goldie and Lisa

Everyone everywhere has all kinds of feelings—just like me.

What about you?

There are many different feelings and many things to know about them.

Let's count our way through the **1-2-3s of feelings** together!

And me!

One thing that connects all people is that we all have feelings.

All our feelings are **okay.**

We feel our feelings in **two** important ways.

We feel them in our bodies and in our minds.

Our bodies may feel hot, shaky, or calm.

Our minds and our thoughts might be telling us we are scared, or excited, or unhappy.

Our feelings come in **three** sizes.

Feelings can be big.

Feelings can be small.

Or feelings can be somewhere in between.

Our feelings change. Here are **four** things to know about feelings:

Feelings are changing all the time.

Feelings give us *information* that helps us decide what to do.

We won't always feel the same way, even about the same things.

Different people have different feelings, even about the same experiences.

Sometimes it can be hard to understand our feelings.

We can understand better when we slow down.

Here are **five** ways to slow down:

Stop what we are doing

Notice our feelings and thoughts

Name the feeling if we can

Breathe and take slow, deep breaths

Take a break and do something different

We can do some or all of these things.

Remember: **Take five!**

We can have lots of feelings at the same time.

It is normal and natural to have many feelings all at once.

Here are **six** pairs of feelings that we might feel together:

★ Nervous and excited

☆ Mad and sad

☆ Bored and lonely

☆ Shy and curious

★ Happy and calm

☆ Afraid and frustrated

What other pairs of feelings can you think of?

Feelings are not right or wrong. They are not good or bad.

Feelings can be comfortable or uncomfortable.

Here are **seven** feelings:

Happy
Sad
Excited
Worried
Calm
Angry
Proud

Here are **seven** more feelings:

Embarrassed
Afraid
Joyful
Lonely
Brave
Jealous
Loved

Which feelings might be comfortable?

Which ones might be uncomfortable?

When a feeling is uncomfortable, we can help ourselves.

We can **talk to ourselves** about our feelings.

I can do it.

Here are **eight** things we could say:

I won't always feel this way.

It's okay to ask for help.

Everyone struggles sometimes.

I can get through this.

I can take care of my feelings.

There is nothing wrong with my feelings.

I am not alone—I can share my feelings.

All of my feelings are okay.

I am trying.

There are even more ways to help ourselves with our feelings.

We can **let them out!**

Here are **nine** ways to let feelings out:

Talk to someone we feel comfortable with.

Act out our feelings in a skit or play.

Write a poem, story, or letter.

Name feelings out loud. Say, "I feel mad." (Or however you feel!)

Cry.

Draw, paint, or make things with clay.

Sing.

Play.

Laugh.

We can also help ourselves with our feelings by . . .

moving our bodies in whatever ways we can.

Here are **ten** physical things to try:

★ Wiggle and stretch.

★ Take three deep breaths.

★ Take a walk or go for a run.

★ Hug a stuffed animal, pet, caring adult, or friend.

★ Jump or skip.

★ Curl up and rest.

★ Squeeze a ball or a pillow.

★ Get outdoors.

★ Dance to music.

★ Play with a toy or game.

Now I know the 1-2-3s
of my many different feelings.

Me too! I know things
to do with my feelings.
I can name them, let them out,
move my body, and more.

What did **you** learn about your feelings?

What will you do to **help yourself** with your feelings?

Talking About Feelings and What to Do with Them: A Guide for Caring Adults

One thing we all have in common is that we all have feelings, and we all need to find ways to manage and deal with them. Our ability to manage our emotions is connected to our effectiveness in navigating the world and creating healthy and supportive relationships with ourselves and others. The earlier we learn how feelings work and what to do with them, the more wellness and life satisfaction we experience.

This guide provides detailed information about the concepts presented in *1-2-3 My Feelings and Me*. This guide can be used to support children in understanding the myriad of emotions they face, how those feelings might be experienced in daily life, and various coping strategies.

1: We All Have Feelings

There is value in knowing and sharing out loud with children that we all have feelings and that we all need to learn how to manage them. All people—including adults—must find ways to deal with comfortable and uncomfortable emotions. The universality of emotional experiences can often be a place of connection and a bridge to creating conversation. Here are some suggested questions to use to engage children as you read the book:

★ "Look at the pictures in the book. How do you think each person is feeling?"

★ "Why do you think that?"

★ "What do you think the person might do about the feelings?"

★ "What else might this person be feeling?"

2: We Can Feel Our Feelings in Two Important Ways

Our feelings can be felt through physical sensations in our body. At the same time, we can experience feelings through thoughts that can fill our mind. Learning how to identify the physical sensations and thoughts we have in response to feelings can help children feel more in charge of their emotions.

Ask children to think about a time when they had feelings filling their bodies and their minds. Ask them questions such as:

★ "What were you feeling?"

★ "Where in your body did you feel it?"

★ "What words did you say to yourself?"

★ "What thoughts filled your head?"

Tell children that learning to ask themselves these questions *while* they are experiencing feelings can help them understand what might be happening and give them ideas about how to handle the situation.

Children may need examples of the physical and cognitive experiences that can accompany emotions. For example, when we are nervous or scared, it may feel like we have butterflies in our stomach, our heart might beat faster, or we may feel hot or out of breath. At the same time, these physical sensations can be accompanied by thoughts such as, "I can't do it," "People will laugh at me," or "Something bad is going to happen." Encourage children to try drawing these feelings, sensations, and thoughts; to act them out; or to write stories about them. These activities may help children become more aware of what is happening for them physically and mentally.

3: Feelings Come in Three Sizes

Feelings (both at the physical and cognitive level) can be felt with various degrees of intensity, from quite small to really big. The intensity of feelings can also change, with bigger feelings decreasing or smaller feelings increasing. It is important to normalize the intensity of the feeling experience for children. Adults can help do this by asking, "How big or strong is this feeling?" and "How long have you been having this feeling?" Adults can also get the conversation going by talking about their own feelings and their intensity. For example, "I was so nervous about going to the dentist that my stomach was hurting" or "I was a little bit frustrated when I could not get my computer working." It is important to help children understand that the size and intensity of feelings gives us information about what's going on inside of us.

It can also be valuable to use a visual scale to display the range of intensity an emotion might have. For instance, you could show children a numeric scale, with 1 representing a low intensity, 5 a medium intensity, and a 10 a high intensity. If this scale were displayed in a classroom or other space, children could then be asked to indicate where on the intensity scale they are feeling during any given situation.

Another way to represent a scale of intensity would be to invite children to draw expressive faces or emojis and then share and describe their drawings. The action of drawing and sharing is a healthy way of exploring and expressing internal emotional experiences. In addition, children could be asked to show with their bodies the different sizes of their feelings. For example, children might stretch their arms wide and make their bodies appear taller and bigger to represent an intense and possibly overwhelming feeling. Children can then be invited to name, as best they can, the strength of the feeling. This will help them get connected physically and mentally to what it feels like to experience this level of emotion. Once the intensity of the feeling is identified, adults can invite children to try various strategies outlined in the book to manage or cope with their feelings.

4: Feelings Are Always Changing

Children and adults will experience many feelings in a single day, a single hour, or even a single minute! Feelings are by nature fluid, constantly growing, lessening, and shifting. Some feelings will change quickly and may be quite easily experienced, processed, and expressed by children and adults. Other feelings will move slowly and need time before they can be articulated. It can be a source of comfort for children to know that no feeling is permanent and their feelings will change. In particular, children may feel better equipped to tolerate emotions—especially strong or uncomfortable emotions—if they understand the experience will not last forever and that feelings are constantly transforming.

Naming these changes when we observe them is one simple, direct, and powerful strategy to help children begin to identify that feelings change. For example, "I noticed this morning you were feeling excited about the soccer game, and now I can see you are feeling a bit nervous" or "You seem to be feeling shy about playing with the other kids at the park. Do you think that feeling may change, and you might feel curious about what they are doing once you are there?" This is not to deny a child's current

feeling experience, but rather support the understanding that things can change. Another way to name and observe children's changing feelings is to chart their moods and feelings over the course of a day or week as a visual display. An additional hands-on strategy, commonly called modeling, is for caring adults to share how our own feelings and reactions change over time.

5: Take Five! Slow Down and Pause

When a child is in the midst of experiencing feelings, it can be helpful and important to slow down and pause. Slowing down and taking some deep breaths can help children figure out what is happening and how they are feeling. Pausing is a strategy that works on both the physical and cognitive aspects of emotional experience. It allows physical sensations to calm and offers some opportunity for clarity about which feelings might be happening. It can lessen children's confusion about what is going on in their bodies and what feelings they may be experiencing. It can also create the possibility of naming and labeling the feelings accurately. This process is essential for both children and adults.

When children slow down and pause, they may find that their feelings lessen or shift. On the other hand, it is also possible that some feelings may intensify for a period of time. It is helpful to understand that stopping to pause is the opposite of avoiding feelings. Rather, it allows room to be with feelings and to process them in a mindful, healthy way.

Breathing is a fundamental part of pausing. Often, when children and adults are experiencing intense feelings, they find that their breath becomes restricted, shallow, or inaccessible. We can sometimes simply forget to breathe deeply. Many deep breathing techniques are available for children to try. For example, in box breathing, the child inhales for a count of four, holds for a count of four, exhales for a count of four, pauses for a count of four, and then begins again. There are many ways to practice deep breathing. Feel free to experiment and find those that work for the child in your life.

6: We Can Have Lots of Feelings at the Same Time

As children develop a better understanding of how feelings work, they benefit from the knowledge that they can feel more than one feeling at a time. It is normal, natural, common, and human to feel many emotions about a single situation. For example, children may feel scared and excited about being faced with a new challenge or experience. These multiple feelings might be similar (such as annoyed, angry, and enraged) or conflicting (such as scared and excited).

Caring adults can help children identify their experience of multiple feelings by asking questions. Some ideas include, "Are you also feeling other feelings right now?" or "I hear you are sad. Are you also feeling disappointed?" We can help children by suggesting a variety of feeling words when describing a situation. For example, "You seem happy, excited, and full of joy about the birthday party."

You can also invite children to play the "AND" game, in which they name a feeling situation such as, "I feel mad when I get interrupted" and you respond by asking an "AND" question such as, "AND what else are you feeling?" The child might respond with mad AND frustrated, annoyed, or tired. You might also ask a child to pick a letter of the alphabet and name as many feeling words as they can that begin with that letter. For example, S is for *scared*, *sad*, *silly*, and *surprised*. You can build on this activity by then naming situations in which the child felt more than one of these feelings. This can highlight for children how many feelings can be experienced together.

7: Feelings Can Be Comfortable or Uncomfortable

Feelings can feel good and be comfortable to experience, or they can feel bad and be a source of discomfort. Children will benefit from knowing that all feelings are a natural part of being human and alive.

One place to start exploring this idea is by talking with children about how some feelings are typically easy and comfortable to experience (joy, happiness, excitement, relief) and others are harder and more uncomfortable (sadness, loneliness, frustration). How we feel our feelings—whether an emotion is experienced as comfortable or uncomfortable—is influenced by our personal history and is unique to each child and adult.

Some concrete ideas for starting a conversation might include working together with children to make a list of feelings that are comfortable to experience and talk about, and a list of those that are uncomfortable and harder to talk about. Another way to explore this is by having children make collages of comfortable and uncomfortable feelings by cutting out pictures from magazines or newspapers. Children could also draw pictures of comfortable or uncomfortable emotions and tell or write stories about them.

8: We Can Talk to Ourselves About Our Feelings

Another helpful and effective strategy to address and manage emotions is to practice the skill of self-talk: having an internal dialogue when we are in the midst of experiencing emotions. This internal dialogue works for a range of feelings and it can be positive, neutral, or negative depending on the person and the situation. Developing positive self-talk and remembering to use it consistently is a skill that often requires patience, practice, and perseverance. Self-talk also offers the possibility for self-acceptance, internal support, and encouragement through difficult experiences.

Talk with children about the idea of self-talk and offer examples of positive self-talk, such as "I can do it," "I am capable," and "I am loved." You can also share examples of neutral self-talk, which might include "These feelings will not last forever" or "I'm doing my best." Encourage practicing this self-talk through a game. Collaborate with children to imagine a scenario and then have children brainstorm examples of positive or neutral self-talk that they might use in this situation. Children could also rate how helpful they feel each statement is. Choosing commonly experienced scenarios such as talking in front of a group, trying out a new activity, or being away from parents can provide real-world context.

Another way to help children practice self-talk is to have them imagine talking to a best or favored friend who is feeling upset or who needs support. Ask, "What kind or helpful words would you tell your friend in this situation?" Children can then move to telling *themselves* these same helpful words.

9: We Can Let Feelings Out

An additional way to manage and cope with a variety of feelings is to express them. Expressing feelings can offer many benefits, such as reduced distress, emotional connectedness, personal clarity, and effective communication. In addition, expressing our feelings allows for a greater understanding of the origins of our specific feelings and experiences.

There are many ways of expressing emotions, such as sharing and talking with (or to) a caring adult, a friend, a pet, or a stuffed animal. Other ways to express emotions include arts and crafts, such as making a collage, journaling, drawing pictures, or acting out feelings in a play or skit.

It's important for children to explore and try out different methods of sharing and expressing feelings to figure out what is most effective for them. Adults can help by guiding children to express themselves in healthy ways that do not harm themselves

or others. It is also important to recognize that the ways of expressing feelings will change as children grow and develop (both physically and emotionally).

10: Moving Our Bodies Can Help with Feelings

Movement and physicality is another way we can address and attend to our feelings. Feelings are a physical experience. When children move their bodies, it can help lower the intensity of their feelings and provide mental clarity about what emotions they're going through.

Some ideas for physical expression include going for a walk or a run, jumping around, riding a bike, having an intense embrace with a parent or other family member, squeezing a pillow, or playing with a favorite game or toy. It is important to figure out what works for children, including those with differing physical abilities or needs, and remembering that what is helpful during one experience may not be as effective during another. Experiment with a wide variety of ideas for physical expression and feel free as caring adults to model this behavior at any time.

What to Do If You Are Concerned About a Child's Emotional Health and Well-Being

If a child regularly displays or discusses extreme feelings or behaviors, or frequently struggles to engage in day-to-day activities, seeking professional help may be needed. In these cases, children and their families may need professional support to move toward emotional health. Caring adults are encouraged to connect with a psychologist, social worker, family physician, or other professional for more information. Seeking help is an important, empowering, and courageous step.

Parting Thoughts

It is helpful for children to know that all feelings are normal and natural. Taking a stance of curiosity toward their experiences and emotions can increase dialogue, sharing, and acceptance. Problem solving can flow more easily when children feel supported and understood. As adults we play a pivotal role in helping children create lifelong emotional wellness, through modeling our own emotional experiences, sharing our internal feeling experiences, and being open and available to children and all their emotions.

Dealing with feelings is a progressive skill. As children gain more practice and support in understanding their multitude of feelings and experiences, they will feel more effective, less overwhelmed, and more capable of dealing with all of life's challenges and celebrations. Remember, we are all in this together!

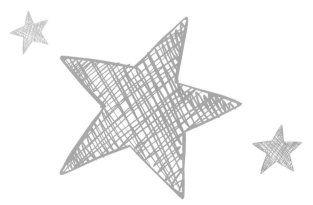

About the Authors and Illustrator

Goldie Millar, Ph.D., is a clinical and school psychologist. She has a deep interest in children's mental health, emotional regulation, mindfulness, and evidence-based intervention strategies. Goldie enjoys reading, painting, and all things outdoors! She lives in Ontario, Canada with her husband and daughters. This is her second children's book. You can find out more about her at 123myfeelingsandme.com and fisforfeelings.com.

Lisa A. Berger, Ph.D., is a clinical, counseling, and rehabilitation psychologist. Her professional interests include emotional health and wellness, psychological trauma, and emotion-based therapy. Lisa is passionate about mountain biking and loves to be in the woods. She enjoys reading and any activity that she engages in with her husband and two daughters. Lisa lives in Ontario, Canada. This is her second children's book. You can find her at 123myfeelingsandme.com and fisforfeelings.com.

Priscilla Burris holds a creative design degree from the Fashion Institute of Design and Merchandising, as well as an early childhood education certificate. She is a member of the Board of Advisors for the Society of Children's Book Writers and Illustrators and is also its US illustrator coordinator and advisor. She lives in Southern California.

Other Great Books from Free Spirit

F Is for Feelings
by Goldie Millar and Lisa A. Berger, illustrated by Hazel Mitchell
For ages 3–8. 40 pp.; PB and HC; color illust.; 11¼" x 9¼".

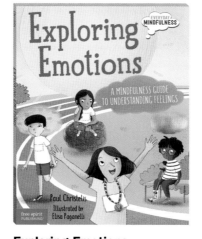

Exploring Emotions
A Mindfulness Guide to Understanding Feelings
by Paul Christelis, illustrated by Elisa Paganelli
For ages 5–9. 32 pp; HC; color illust.; 7½" x 9".
Free Leader's Guide freespirit.com/leader

Gentle Hands and Other Sing-Along Songs for Social-Emotional Learning
by Amadee Ricketts, illustrated by Ashley Barron
For ages 3–8. 32 pp.; HC; color illust.; 11¼" x 9¼"; includes downloadable sheet music for all songs.

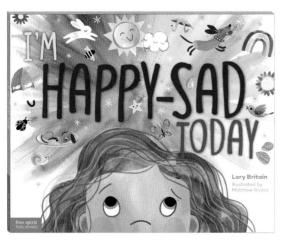

I'm Happy-Sad Today
Making Sense of Mixed-Together Feelings
by Lory Britain, Ph.D., illustrated by Matthew Rivera
For ages 3–8. 40 pp.; HC; color illust.; 11¼" x 9¼".

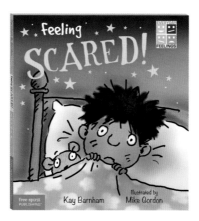

Feeling Scared!
by Kay Barnham, illustrated by Mike Gordon
For ages 5–9. 32 pp.; HC; color illust.; 7½" x 8¼".
Free Leader's Guide freespirit.com/leader

For pricing information, to place an order, or to request a free catalog, contact:

Free Spirit Publishing
6325 Sandburg Road • Suite 100
Minneapolis, MN 55427-3674
toll-free 800.735.7323
local 612.338.2068
fax 612.337.5050
help4kids@freespirit.com
freespirit.com